RACE AGAIN

The Power of Faith and Family

Ronnie Weller

Race Again by Ronnie Weller

ISBN-13: 978-0692409060

ISBN-10: 0692409068

Printed in the United States of America

Unless otherwise noted all scripture is from The Holy Bible

Library of Congress Control Number: 2015938194
MACKEY PRODUCTIONS, ROOSEVELT, NEW YORK

🏁

**Race Again,
Believe Again,
Walk Again,
Laugh, Love,
and Learn Again.**

TABLE OF CONTENTS

![checkered flag] DEDICATION

To God, Our Father, who has given me the greatest gifts in life: knowing You, loving You, and trusting You and for believing in Our Lord Jesus Christ and The Holy Spirit. And for giving me my two most precious gifts here on earth......my loving sons, Jimmy and John.

To Jim, my wonderful and supportive husband.

To my amazing sons who bring joy to my life every day!

ACKNOWLEDGEMENTS

It was truly The Holy Spirit who guided me and encouraged me to write this for which I will always be grateful.

It is impossible for me to thank and acknowledge all of you who have supported and prayed for our family, but please know you are all so very special to us and will always remain in our hearts. We can never thank all of you enough.

To Jeff McCall, Jimmy's crew chief at the time, for believing in our son enough to take him to the next level of racing and for helping us get through the most difficult time of our lives. We love ya!

To the Push Truck Driver who quickly drove us across the track to get to our son.

To Jerry Keminski, the lead Paramedic who did everything in his power to save our son; to Tommy Williams and all of the track crew who worked so hard to get him out of that racecar.

To Lauri Eberhart.

To the Helicopter Pilot and crew.

To Dr. Joe Bernard, Dr. Frederick Finger, Dr. Jerry Petty and Dr. Terry Trammel.

To all the Nurses, Doctors and Staff at Carolina's Medical Center and Rehabilitation Hospital.

To Father Larry who was the Priest at CMC Rehabilitation Hospital while we were there.

To Chad Wagner, Linda Barlow and Quaker Steak and Lube of Sharon, PA for putting on a wonderful benefit and for all who volunteered to work at the benefit in making it a huge success!

To all the wonderful people who attended, who donated beautiful baskets, gifts and monetary gifts for Jimmy's benefit to help with the medical bills.

To NASCAR driver Dave Blaney and his family; to all the NASCAR drivers who donated amazing memorabilia for the auction and the wonderful autographed gifts they sent to Jimmy.

To Msgr. Robert Siffrin of St. Edward Parish, Youngstown, Ohio. Thank you for inviting Jimmy to speak at the church and take pictures there.

To all of our dearest family, friends and racing community for all the prayers, love, support and hard work; and for everyone who made the long trips to Charlotte or to our house to visit Jimmy and our family in show of support.

To my good friend Fannie Jackson for introducing me to Pastor Arthur Mackey.

Thank you Pastor Arthur Mackey for all the hard work and dedication you have given to make this book possible. May God continue to bless you and your family.

May God bless all of you!

FOREWORD

Ever since I was little, I was taught that God puts people into our lives for a reason. That reason was never fully understood until the time that followed my accident on October 13, 2004. It was a night that started out as a dream come true for me, but ended in a way that would change not only my life, but everyone's close to me forever.

I have always told everyone that I was on the easy side of the accident. Sure, I experienced the physical pains that night and every day since, but it cannot compare to the emotional and mental pains that my family has experienced. To see a loved one strapped into a car and hanging in the fence, lifeless, and then having to fight for their life in the weeks to follow, takes a special kind of person.

Having God's blessing and Jesus' blood poured out upon me, a sinner, that night, and me being able to get back to living the life I only dreamed about being able to obtain, is an act of love greater than most men ever have or will experience. I have never been afraid to tell of this great love to anyone who was down or questioning their faith, but I wished I was able to do more. Even speaking to youth groups didn't seem to be accomplishing what God kept me on this earth to do; bring people to Him and let them feel His love. It may sound crazy, but I feel my family and I were blessed to be put in this situation. We are able to tell a story of God's undying love, and if as little as one person can be saved and brought closer to God, all the pain and suffering was well worth it.

I have seen all the hard work and pain that my mom has gone through to get our story down on paper, and I am very proud of her. It takes a special woman to be able to get her family through such a tragedy and never lose or even have her faith in God shaken. I thank God for the awesome family and friends that He has blessed me with, and I hope hearing my mom's side of the story will bring you to a deeper understanding of God and Jesus' perfect love for us.

- **Jimmy Weller, NASCAR Driver**

CHAPTER 1
NOT MINE HIS

IN GOD'S HANDS

Growing up as a child, I remember my Mother, who endeared many hardships, taught me a valuable lesson – leave it in God's Hands. It took many years and a family of my own to truly understand the real meaning. Even as a child my faith had always been strong, so I thought.

How would I know that one day, my faith would prove to be stronger than I had ever imagined and be blessed with the greatest gift ever?

Whenever I couldn't sleep, I would always remember many nights as a young girl going downstairs to witness my Mom sitting on the couch alone reading The Bible. My Mother really never talked too much about religion; but I always felt her faith was deep inside her. She made sure we always went to church, attended Catholic school, and that we made all of our Sacraments. I always knew our Lord was a very important part of our life, especially my own, but I still didn't realize how much.

When my husband Jim and I were married, we shared that same faith I cherished so much. Not only were we blessed with a wonderful marriage, we were also blessed with two wonderful and amazing children.

As the kids grew up, we spent a lot of time at the dirt race tracks. My husband drove a big block modified car every weekend. Jim included the boys in so much of the racing that they loved every bit of it.

We did a lot of praying at our house, especially for Jim's safety on the track. You see, I learned to put Jim in God's hands so I could handle him racing, but the thought of my boys doing it was altogether different. Our first son, Jimmy of course, loved racing. Everything growing up was – "let's see how fast I could do this" from picking up his toys to getting dressed, to cleaning his room. Every school report had something to do with racing. Everything he did had to be timed, it was truly a racing game, which, by the way, came in pretty handy when we needed to get things done. He literally lived it in everything he did. His dream was to be a great race car driver.

Here's where it all started for Jimmy: the local tracks we raced at would have the kids from age 2 (on big wheels) to, I believe, 16 race their bicycles on the front straightaway of the track. Jimmy won quite a few trophies back then. A little piggy bank filled with pennies was his very first trophy. We still have that trophy! And that is how his racing career got started. He was so cute, he wore a little blue race suit and a plastic helmet (he was the only one dressed in full race gear). He took his racing very seriously even at the age of two! Then he moved on to racing go karts for a few years starting at the age of seven until he was old enough to race one of his Dad's cars.

Then came my greatest fear; he would now be racing cars at the age of 15. Seeing him in a racecar was exciting, but truly very frightening. I have watched my husband race for many years, but, nothing compares to when your child goes out on the track for the first time.

Believing my faith was strong enough to get me through this and remembering those valuable words my mother taught me as a child, Leave it in God's Hands, is exactly what I had to do.

In all honesty, it worked! As nervous as I was,
I trusted God enough to know my son would
be safe and that I too, would be okay.

After racing two years in the Modified, winning several heat races and coming so close to winning the main feature several times until the last race of that season, Jimmy finally gets his win...a huge feature win! He was now ready to get behind the wheel of a 410 Sprint car, the ones with the wings on top. Sprint cars are so much faster than the Modifieds, and to me so much more dangerous...but that being said from a Mom's point of view, not the guys! Actually, they really are safe.

This is Jimmy's first win in the Modified compliments of Joe Secka - JMS Pro Photo

He had several heat wins and several feature wins. He loved every bit of racing the sprint cars and really wanted to make a career out of racing these cars for a number of years. He kept telling us how much fun they were. He loved those Sprint cars and racing on dirt!

After a year and a half of racing and several flips in the sprint car, (walking away from them all and thanking God every time), we were so proud of him for doing so well in his racing, but mostly for Jimmy always thanking God for giving him the opportunity to race, believing in himself and for fulfilling a dream he lived for.

Here is where, I believe my faith begins to be tested: On October 13, 2004, we were at the Lowe's Motor Speedway in Charlotte, NC. Jimmy was going to race in the USAC wingless Sprint show. He had just finished his first season running a 410 Sprint car, which I was told was supposed to be much faster than the wingless Sprint cars. So my fears, let's just say, weren't as bad.

Nothing seemed unusual at the time. I prayed as I always do, hugging my boys to the point they were probably getting tired of it (just putting up with it because they knew how nervous I get at the track).

With my faith being as strong as ever, I put my trust in Jesus and put my son in God's hands. Everything was good.

Everyone was so excited and anxious to get the race started—especially Jimmy. He was so happy. At one point before the races started, he and I had to go and get gas down the road. All he could talk about was how much it meant to him to be there to run that race and how grateful he was that he was given this opportunity. At this point, he had said several prayers throughout the day, which hadn't surprised me at all. Both our boys have always felt a closeness to Our Lord and always felt the need to go to Church every Sunday, no matter how far away from home they were (even when we weren't with them). They always set aside time for prayer and reading The Bible. We always taught them that you must love God with all your heart and soul and believe and trust in Jesus.

Before the practices, Jimmy and I went to grab a hamburger; anyone knowing Jimmy knows he has to have something to eat right before he gets into the car...sometimes still eating as he's buckling in. We just laugh. It was then that I asked him, "Are you okay doing this?" and he looked up at me with such contentment and love and said..."Mom, this is so much fun! I can't thank you and Dad enough."

I was so proud of him. You see, he is not only my child; he is God's child; He's my child temporarily; he's God's child for eternity. Not Mine – His.

A PARENT'S WORST NIGHTMARE!

Practice went well and then came the heat races. As Jimmy was pulling out onto the track, my heart was pounding so fast and my stomach had that usual nervous feeling, nothing unusual. I had no need to worry. God was with him, he had the safest race car, all the best safety equipment and the best helmet. Everything was just right. My faith was strong...only God knew our lives were about to change dramatically...traumatically! Around 8:00 that evening the heat races began. Jimmy was leading when a caution came out, stopping the race. When the race restarted, he got pushed back to third place. As Jimmy was entering turn one to take over second place he hit a large rut in the tracks surface, which threw him violently into the wall. Flipping horribly several times and hitting head on into the cement pole in the catch fence and ending up in the fence several feet in the air.

There was not one sound in the entire place.

Krista Voda of FOX Sports 1 reported that, "Charlotte Motor Speedway sits at the intersection of Highway 29 and Bruton Smith Boulevard. Right across the street is the dirt track. Ten years ago, an 18-year-old driver named Jimmy Weller was at that track to race. He walked in, he did not walk out."[1]

I knew in my heart this crash was like no other he had been involved in. I can never express in words what I was feeling. It's a parent's worst nightmare!

Charlotte Speedway Grand Counsel Lauri Eberhart stated in an interview with FOX Sports 1, "I was in the control tower, and all of a sudden we saw this horrific wreck. So, we saw the car coming into the fourth turn, catch the rut with the tire, and then flip, you know, ten to 15 times. I don't remember how many times it was, but flipped, over and over again."[2]

---

[1] FOX Sports 1, Krista Voda, May 16, 2014

[2] FOX Sports 1 interview with Laura Eberhart on May 16, 2014.

The Crash

The Crash

The Crash

The Crash

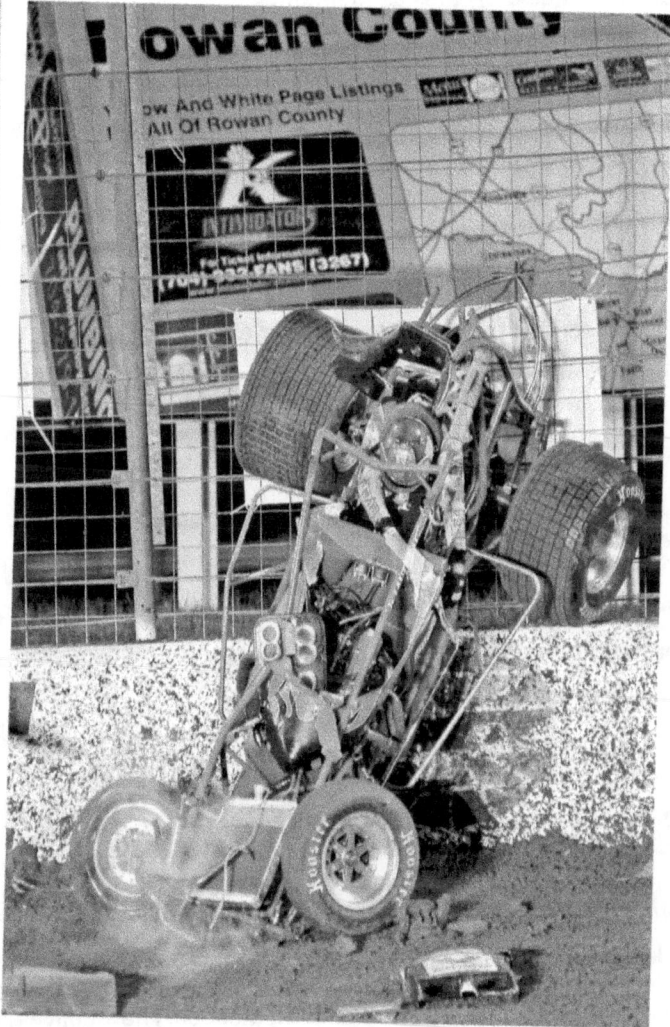

I felt so lifeless and so helpless. My husband and I, our younger son, John, Chris Chaky (our Godson), and Jeff McCall (Jimmy's crew chief), were watching from turns 3 and 4. Jim and I ran to the nearest push truck, and the driver immediately took us to Jimmy.

When we got out of the truck and ran to where Jimmy was, we literally collapsed in fear and devastation. Praying to God with everything I had inside of me – I wasn't going to let go of the strong faith and love for God that I knew I had always relied on.

As I looked up and saw my beautiful, loving son so lifeless, I begged the EMT in my weakest voice…"Please let me hold my son…he's scared… he's alone…he needs me." And at that very moment, I looked up at my son…Jesus was on one side…and Mary was on the other…holding our son.

At the most horrific moment of my life I felt a sense of peace and calmness, and I knew, whatever happens my son was not alone. The trust I had always placed in our Lord Jesus meant everything. It wasn't until later that I realized that the faith I had always known was stronger than I had ever imagined.

How could I find peace at the very moment when our whole lives had stopped? When nothing else mattered?

By the Grace of God I witnessed the most beautiful, fulfilling site that I had ever laid eyes on! What did I do to deserve such a wonderful gift?

This is all I had to hold onto, and from that moment on, I never once gave up hope, I never once questioned God; I never got angry with Him; and I never blamed Him. I just thanked Him for every precious moment that our son was holding on.

Romans 5:1 declares and decrees that, "Therefore being justified by faith, we have peace with God through our Lord Jesus Christ:..."

Mike Hembree wrote an article concerning Jimmy in the *USA TODAY* Sports section special dated June 2, 2014 and said of the day of Jimmy's crash, "The image of her son hanging limp in the shattered remains of his race car — his face a moribund shade of blue — still brings tears to Ronnie Weller's eyes." Hembree went on to write, "The crash happened in a United States Auto Club sprint-car race at the Dirt Track at Charlotte Motor Speedway on Oct. 13, 2004. Without the quick and decisive action of numerous individuals, Jimmy Weller III would have died that night. It was a clear and cool autumn evening, one that changed the lives of Weller and everyone in his family circle — and his racing circle — forever."[3]

At that point no one could even tell us if Jimmy was even breathing the slightest breath of air.

---

[3] Mike Hembree, *USA TODAY* Sports section special, June 2, 2014.

The EMT's worked diligently with every effort they had to rescue him. I completely lost everything inside of me when I saw them put a white sheet over our son. We had no idea, until later, the reason why they did that; they did not want the fans and media to see them working on him. The helicopter arrived within minutes. Quickly, the track officials put us into a vehicle that was waiting on the track for us so that we could be at the hospital when the helicopter arrived.

At that time, Jimmy was 18 and just out of high school, and John was 15. My heart was literally breaking. Jimmy told FOX Sports 1, "I know how hard it was on them. And I could see the tears in my mom's eyes when we do talk about it. Mom said when I was hanging in the fence, she actually saw Jesus and Mary holding me, so that comfort that she had knowing no matter what happened, I wasn't alone."[4]

John needed us just as much as Jimmy did. At this point, he thought he lost his brother, his best friend.

To him, Jimmy had died, and in turn part of him had died, as it did in all of us. My son Johnny said to FOX Sports 1, "I thought it was over really, I mean it was...it was kind of hard to,...to absorb, because I had no idea. I was by myself at the time,...so, a little hard to take in."[5]

---

[4] FOX Sports 1 interview with Jimmy Weller on May 16, 2014.
[5] Ibid.

**My husband, Johnny and I could not give up hope.
The ride to the hospital had to be
the longest ride I had ever been on.**

Lauri Eberhart who had worked for the track drove us to the hospital. I still can't imagine how she was able to offer us so much comfort while we were all so devastated. She was there for us, and we will always be grateful to her. Truly a blessing!

There was tremendous silence in that half hour ride. All three of us were unaware of each others' presence.

**We were all so focused on Jimmy and praying to God,
the only One we knew who could help us.**

I was saying the Rosary as fast, but as sincere and intense as I ever had when something happened...it felt like...like...all the life had been sucked out of me and there was an incredible calm feeling along with the most intense brightness...lasting only seconds.

JESUS, MARY, AND JIMMY - HOPE, STRENGTH and COURAGE

It was then that I knew Jimmy was going to be okay. I'll never truly be able to explain what I had just experienced. I just knew we were not alone, because I felt the presence of God. Every minute that went by I was completely focused on Jesus, Mary and Jimmy; my hope, my strength and my courage.

I had to be strong for both John and Jimmy. My faith is what was holding me together.

We arrived at the hospital before the helicopter which wasn't right, knowing that it was only a seven minute flight. Finding out later that the reason was because the EMTs were still working on him at the track, and God bless all of them for giving everything that they had to work on our son! Still not giving up on the only hope I had – Our Lord. We sat in the waiting room waiting to find out something, anything...!

The three of us were hurting so badly that we didn't even have the strength to comfort one another.

It seemed like forever as we sat there waiting until they arrived with our son. When they did, still no one could give us any answers. As of this point, we had no idea whether our son was alive or not.

> I only had my faith and what I had
> witnessed to keep me from falling apart.

We were taken to the Carolina Medical Center waiting room right outside the Intensive Care Unit in the Trauma Center where we met with the doctor. I can only imagine what he was feeling as he tried to comfort us while at the same time he had to tell us our son's breathing was very shallow. Jimmy was in a coma, and he had traumatic brain injury - the worst kind. He also had facial fractures, a broken neck and broken vertebras in his back and two collapsed lungs.

> I know why Dr. Bernard was our son's doctor.
> He was very sympathetic to our fears and
> very compassionate in explaining everything to us.
> I truly believe he felt our pain.

PAIN & PRAYER

Dr. Bernard had explained to us that Jimmy had severe bleeding of the brain, tiny tares were all through it and that they would have to put a probe in his head to monitor the swelling. I was so weak from crying; we all were. All we could do was put our trust in Jesus and pray. We couldn't give up. By this time, word had gotten out to all of our family and friends everywhere. It was all over the news, in Charlotte and back home in Ohio and all over the Internet...and, thank God it was, because everyone everywhere was praying.

You see, Jimmy is a very special young man with a huge heart. He loves people, and he loves God.

While he was just starting out racing the sprint car, Jeff, his crew chief was running the Dave Blaney Sprint Car School and part of the school included a ride in the two seater sprint car. Well, before Jimmy ever had his first Sprint car race, Jeff let him give the rides in the two seater car...which scared me to death! He had never even raced them yet!!!! I asked him..."Jimmy, do you tell the people (before they pay for this), that you have never even raced these yet before they get into the car with you?????" He said, "Yeah, Mom, I tell them before they get in, but I think they think I'm just kidding, and they say they'll go anyway." And, from all the cards (over 800) we received from all over, the people who had taken rides with Jimmy all commented on what a wonderful young man he was, mentioning his warm smile and how grateful they were to have met him. God bless all of them!

Just to put this in perspective, when it came to his first sprint car race at the East Bay Race Track in Florida, the school was going on at the track before the races began. The track was having a tribute to Lyn St. James, an Indy car driver, who was to get a ride with Jimmy in the two seater...boy, was I afraid to meet her afterwards, because believe me... I wouldn't get in the car with him or at least not until he had a few years under him...mmm, maybe not even then because I know he would have done everything he could to scare the heck out of me!

One summer, my boys had bought me a wonderful Mother's Day present, a ride in the two seater with Dave Blaney at Sharon Speedway, and...let me tell you...it was better than any roller coaster ride I was ever on. It was very scary and exciting, but he also was a trained professional race car driver, and, yes, I would definitely do it again. With my son, no!!! You have no control, only the driver does.

Well...before Jimmy gave Lyn St. James her ride it was announced over the speaker at the track, and everyone was watching. Not me, I was too scared...I just prayed!!!!!

Afterwards, we had the honor to meet Lyn, what a remarkable lady. She couldn't say enough nice things about Jimmy. What really made me laugh is that she told us, had she known he had never done this before, she would have never gotten in the car, BUT...she was glad she did. He did great! She even mentioned all of that in an article they did about her. He thought that was pretty awesome! When she heard of Jimmy's accident, she immediately sent him a beautiful card with an autograph picture to the hospital and told him that she was keeping him in her prayers. We were so touched and so grateful for all the prayers and cards we received.

So you see, Jimmy had touched so many lives that it would be so hard to imagine him not being here anymore. He had so much love to give.

Romans 12:12 states,
"Rejoicing in hope; patient in tribulation;
continuing instant in prayer,"

After the doctor had left, all we could do was pray and not give up hope. Everyone was praying, and thank God they were. Dr. Bernard came to see us in the early morning hours and looked at us with a look of no other - he told us...the bleeding has dissipated...

He explained to us that he had done all he could, and it was out of his hands, and that he truly believed that God took over. He explained to us that when things like this happen, things that cannot be explained, that IS the only answer.

What an amazing, faith-filled doctor to give the credit to Our Lord. I believe that Jesus guided his every move as he worked on our son. Thank God for his faith.

I truly believe the man that he is, the Doctor that he has become, he will truly be successful in everything his does. He is truly blessed, and I pray that if we were ever in a situation like that again, we would have the honor of having another doctor like him. We will always be grateful to him, and he will always remain in our prayers.

I wish I could explain the feelings that were going through all of us; we had hope; thank you God; thank you Lord Jesus.

We were now able to go in to see Jimmy for only a few minutes. As I walked quietly into the Trauma Center ICU unit (it only had, I believe, 4 or 5 beds with the worst kind of injury patients, an image that will never ever leave me), my whole body felt so empty, but yet so willing to see my son. He was in the second bed and I...I couldn't believe that was my son...he was hooked to every possible machine. He had a ventilator, two tubes running in each side of his chest, a neck brace on, his little head and face were so swollen, unrecognizable...and a horrible color of black & blue. His eyes were so, so swollen shut. He laid there so lifeless. If it wasn't for my heart knowing that that was Jimmy, I would have never believed it. As I reached his bed, I gently, ever so gently touched his hand and fell to my knees; all I wanted to do was hug him. I was crying. I tried not to, but the tears just kept coming.

I truly believed that he was alive and he could hear me and sense that we were there.

I knew that he was going to be ok;
God had given that to me.
This is where my faith truly grew even beyond my limits.

My husband was on one side of Jimmy and I was on the other. John stayed at the base of his bed. All we could do was pray. We prayed with everything that we had in us. Those few minutes were gone, it was time leave. I couldn't leave him; I didn't want to leave him.

I gently reached over him without touching him,
wanting so desperately to hold him, and whispered
to him how much I loved him and that
we were never going to leave him.

I let him know that he was not alone, Jesus and Mary were right there with him. That was the only way that I could leave my son in that room without us.

James 5:15 states,
"And the prayer of faith shall save the sick,
and the Lord shall raise him up; and if he have
committed sins, they shall be forgiven him."

Tomi, his nurse, an amazing young girl, knew we didn't want to leave. She gave us so much comfort knowing that they were going to do everything that they could to save our son. His condition was very, very critical. Every second that he held on was very critical to his surviving. Tomi was incredibly compassionate in her job, which we were so grateful for. The ICU room was very quiet and had to be kept with very low lighting. The atmosphere for the trauma patients had to be very calm. It would have been very dangerous for them to get upset or excited. We knew we had to leave so they could finish prepping Jimmy; we knew how extremely important their job was.

Tomi assured us that she would tell us immediately when we could get back in to see Jimmy. God had truly worked through all the doctors and nurses at this facility. They were amazing. As we walked out of the room, we couldn't even speak; we just quietly kept to ourselves. I cried and I prayed. There are no words that could ever express how we felt. It wasn't too long after they got Jimmy all settled that we were able to go back in and see him.

My heart was breaking knowing that I couldn't even touch my son for fear of hurting him...it took everything I had not to hold him and never let go.

My husband and I quietly reached over him, John staying as close to us as he could and we prayed The Our Father, The Hail Mary and The Glory Be, each and every time we got to see him. I will explain later how important it was and what an impact it had. As I mentioned before, even though he was in a coma, I believe with all my heart...he knew...he knew we were there. He knew how much we all loved him, and we would be there by his side no matter what. As you could imagine, the doctor's had no idea what the long term affect from the brain injury would be. They didn't know if he would ever walk again let alone think or look the same as he did. It didn't matter to the three of us what the outcome would be. We loved Jimmy so much that nothing would keep us from helping our son live the rest of his life the way God had meant it to be. Paralyzed, handicapped, blind, whatever the prognosis was, we were willing to do whatever it took to keep him with us.

You see, love has no boundaries, no limits, as long as you put God first. You must love God with all your heart and all your soul and truly believe that Jesus loves each and every one of us.

There were days of no movement, no reaction, nothing...then one day, when I held Jimmy's hand, as I always did, it was different...when I told him I loved him he had the slightest movement, one that I will never forget, ever! The nurse was right there, by his side, every second which enabled her to witness this movement. She felt that it was an involuntary reaction that happens to brain injury patients, not necessarily the reaction I wanted it to be. But, I believe my son reacted with love...he knew. I truly believe that with all my heart. As days went on we saw little, but major movements. Praise God! Praise Jesus!

Tomi was unbelievable; God truly picked her for the job she does. She kept us informed about everything that was going on. She was very sensitive to Jimmy's injuries as she checked on him. All the nurses there treated him as if they knew where he hurt and how to keep him comfortable.

They took their job very seriously and compassionately. And when it came to our feelings, they treated us as if we were their own family.

CHAPTER 2

What a Miracle!

WHAT A MIRACLE!

A week later, another nurse, Shannon, was there. She came outside the ICU room to the room right outside the door that we hadn't ever left yet...and asked to talk to us. She wanted us to know that she was on duty the night they brought our son in. She told us that when she went home that night, she cried; it really touched her that a young man that age that had so much of his life ahead of him, wasn't going to make it. It really struck her, you see, she was not much older than Jimmy. AND...when she came in that day and saw that Jimmy was still there, she couldn't believe it. She was so happy that she couldn't wait to meet us and tell us what she had witnessed. What a miracle! She was soooo adorable. My husband would often whisper to him..."Jimmy, you just gotta wake up... you really have to meet Shannon!!!"

The next time Jim and I were able to go in and see our son, we both held each one of his hands and whispered to him that we loved him, and the most amazing thing happened...he...he squeezed our hands so very, very gently. I cried. I couldn't hold back the tears, they were tears of joy and there was no holding them back.

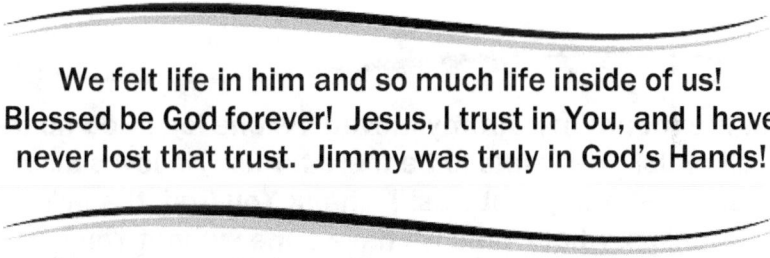

We felt life in him and so much life inside of us! Blessed be God forever! Jesus, I trust in You, and I have never lost that trust. Jimmy was truly in God's Hands!

As I have been writing this, I have cried, I have felt the pain all over again, and, at this very moment, I feel the presence of God and I am as excited as I was that very day.

Every day after that, we were given so many movements and so many signs...what a miracle! Every sign was as special as the last.

As Jimmy started to show progress, they kept him in an induced coma for fear of his neck and the brain injury. They were real protective of even the slightest move of his neck; this was still a very critical situation. They explained to us how dangerous it would be if he were to move his neck the wrong way or if someone would bump it...everyone was very careful as not to bump him at all!

Now, Jimmy was still very weak and was not getting any movement in his legs as of yet and they had mentioned that there was a great possibility that he wasn't getting any movement because of the vertebras in his back pressing on his spinal cord; he could very well never walk again. Here's another time that my faith had to pull us through. We all definitely started praying, actually we never quit. I do believe the nurses were also praying. I promised God that we would always take care of Jimmy no matter what. The doctor was very concerned about this and was going to quickly schedule more tests.

In the meantime, Jimmy moved his one leg...God hears all of us! He wants to be there for us. He loves all of us. What a day that was!!! Thank You God, thank You Jesus, what would we have done without You?

Acts 17:28
declares and decrees and I believe that,
"For in Him we live, and move, and have our being;"

As time went on, they tried two different times to take the ventilator out, but Jimmy was too weak to breathe on his own yet. Then finally, one day he did.

You see, we have had so many blessings from the minute Jimmy got hurt. And remember I mentioned about how our praying over Jimmy really worked and how it made an incredible impact?

Well, when we went into see him after the ventilator was out, he was still not awake, and Jim and I did the first thing we always did, we starting praying over Jimmy with the nurses right there beside us and we noticed that Jimmy's mouth was moving ever so slowly as if he was saying something. We all looked at each other; Jim and I bent down so close to his face (our loving child's terribly bruised and swollen face)...he was saying The Our Father and The Hail Mary...I always believed he knew we were there and he could hear us. And I believe in my heart he knew Jesus and Mary were right there with him. This was proof. The nurses and the doctor who were at hand ready to put the ventilator back in just in case, had just witnessed something incredible. We all did! It was something so spiritual -something so unexplainable!

How could anyone lose faith? You can't! I know sometimes things get very hard for us to cope with, but I can honestly tell you Our Lord will never leave or forsake us.

Hebrews 13:5 states,
"Let your conversation be without covetousness; and be content with such things as ye have: for he hath said, I will never leave thee, nor forsake thee."

Jesus gave us strength and courage. Strength we never thought we had. We hadn't even eaten, maybe a cracker or two in a week and half, hadn't slept, hardly talked, but we were there for each other.

The doctor said we had to keep our strength up because Jimmy was going to need all the help we could give him. Hearing Jimmy, well, kind of hearing, mostly reading Jimmy's lips praying, gave us all the energy we needed.

Thank God we never gave up. You can't.

When I am done writing this, if I can only bring one person closer, or back to God, I have done God's work. Everyone must realize, and I know it's hard, believe me, I know it isn't easy, but they must realize that through some tragedy, some trauma, through something horrible, there is always a blessing. It may not come right away, but it will!

I feel I can say that because of Jimmy's accident. He has brought a lot of people closer to God.

Jimmy has built a stronger relationship with Jesus and more admiration toward the Blessed Mother, as we all have.

We received a call one day from a customer who does business with my husband and who is also a very good friend. I can remember to this day when Sam called. He told me in a very sincere, shaken voice that he couldn't remember when the last time he had prayed so hard... and...that he has been on his knees praying for our son. He loves our boys, and it affected him deeply as it did everyone who knew Jimmy. No one could imagine that this happened to Jimmy. I have great respect for Sam for letting his feelings show so deeply. It took courage to make that call as I'm sure it did for everyone who tried to get a hold of us. Jim and I can honestly say that we never felt alone, we actually felt the presence of everyone back home. I know that sounds a little strange...but, it's true.

For all the people that we heard from and all the people that made the long trips to Charlotte, we will always be grateful. Thank you and may God bless all of you.

Race Again,
Believe Again,
Walk Again,

Laugh, Love,
and Learn Again.

THE POWER OF LOVE

Jimmy was now going to be moved to a step down ICU unit. He was slowing coming out of the induced coma and as we were told, when brain injury patients come out of it, even if it's for seconds, or minutes, they always think it's the first time they wake up and want everything off of them...monitors, the neck brace anything that is foreign to them. It was quite the struggle for all of us. Every time he woke up, he would be so agitated and would thrash terribly.

Anyone who has ever witnessed this knows the horrible sense of helplessness a person feels when you see your loved one go through this; ESPECIALLY when it's your own child. Thank God Jim and I were there with him. We always tried to do our best to calm him down. I tried, but I wasn't as good at it as my husband was. I think my emotions would always get in the way; Jimmy probably could sense that I wasn't very good at holding back the tears. Jim would just take his hand and gently rub Jimmy's face and talk very calmly to him until he calmed down.

It was the most amazing show of a father's love I had ever seen; so tender, so patient...so much love. I have always admired my husband, but, this act of unselfishness he showed goes way beyond admiration.

Now, this would happen quite frequently, and sometimes it would take up to ten minutes to get Jimmy to finally relax. It was very exhausting for all of us, but it was so much better for Jimmy because as long as we were there and could calm him, they would not have to sedate him or tie his hands down. Through all of this, my love for my husband grew stronger and stronger. He was so amazing and so loving with our son (as he always was).

I thanked God that we were there together; we were never apart and this made our relationship stronger than ever.

We both love our boys just as much as the other one does, and we were not going to let our son go through this alone.

GOD'S PLAN FOR US

I need to mention that Beth, one of the nurses that helped us, and her husband were a couple we knew from back home. Coincidence – I don't think so! It just plays in on all of God's plans for us. After Jimmy made his first movement, Beth and another wonderful nurse, Mimi, had arranged for us to have a family waiting room to be our own private room for a few days. They took good care of us. Beth and her husband, Don, did everything they could to make sure we had whatever we needed.

**They will never know how much we truly
appreciate everything they did for us!!!
Thank you God for putting them in our lives.**

Jeremiah 29:11 states,
"For I know the plans I have for you," declares the Lord,
"plans to prosper you and not to harm you,
plans to give you hope and a future."

Everyone took good care of Jimmy like he was their own, and I believe that was such a big part in his recovery. Also, adding that the doctors and nurses told Jim and I he would never have been this far if it weren't for us being there with him, the patience that we had, and the love we have for him. Why wouldn't we have? He was our child, our gift from God. We could never leave him.

God gave us our families; we must never let God down. We must be there for them, no matter what the circumstance is. We must never take them for granted or leave them when they need us the most.

In the step down unit, Mike, his nurse went beyond the call of duty as they all did. He was determined to get Jimmy out of there and on to the Rehab Hospital. Jimmy related to him very well, he was a huge race fan and they talked guy stuff. Well, let's just say, Mike talked, Jimmy listened. They really did communicate, I guess the nurses have to be really trained to understand how trauma patients are coping with everything.

I was so glad that we were at this facility. Amazing! Another Blessing!

By this time, Jimmy started to slowly open his eyes. When he could open them about halfway we couldn't believe what we saw, they were so black & blood stained inside. I couldn't believe it. I was sick to my stomach, not because of how his eyes looked, it was because I could only imagine how much pain my son endured. I wondered if he would ever be able to see again. Mike kept reassuring us as time goes on they will heal.

He was right; as the swelling from the brain and his face and eyes started to go down, he was beginning to look like himself. I want to go into more detail about how horrifying this all was, but I can't. I can only tell you some of it because of how important it is for everyone to understand how loving and compassionate Our Lord is. He can do anything. As you will see with Jimmy's progress you will know that Jesus performs any and all miracles as long as we have faith.

There is nothing our Lord can't do. I promise.

Jimmy was in this ICU for about a week and a half, and then he was moved to another step down unit which enabled us to spend every minute of the day with him. We were literally able to take part in his healing; we cared for him, changed him, fed him, we did whatever we could. It was the most rewarding experience ever! We all have to understand that whatever happens...it's God's will. And we have to be able to accept it, whatever the outcome is. We may not understand it, but we have to have faith and believe in Him.

Our God is a Loving God;
He doesn't want any of us to suffer.

People have often told us, they can't understand why this happened to Jimmy, he's a good kid and he didn't deserve this.

All I could tell them was, we don't understand why things happen, but I know that Jesus suffered more than any of us will ever suffer.

Isaiah 53:5 says,
"But he was wounded for our transgressions, he was bruised for our iniquities: the chastisement of our peace was upon him; and with his stripes we are healed."

Jesus is God's Son. Jesus suffered for ALL of us. I believe that no matter how bad things are, if we still love God with all our heart, He will bring us through even the worst of the worst. If we didn't have pain and suffering, we would never be able to appreciate what Heaven is all about. There is no pain and suffering in Heaven; Jesus has taught us that through all of His teachings.

We have to believe. We must always remember that faith is believing and not seeing. I know that my faith has truly been tested - I just pray that I have passed.

James 1:3 states,
"Knowing this, that the trying of
your faith worketh patience."

Little by little, the machines came off; Jimmy was more and more alert.
He still wasn't able to talk yet, but we still communicated very well.

**When you love someone,
you don't always need words to express it.**

Ecclesiastes 9:11

I returned, and saw under the sun,

that the race is not to the swift, nor the battle to

the strong, neither yet bread to the wise, nor yet

riches to men of understanding,

nor yet favour to men of skill;

but time and chance happeneth to them all.

CHAPTER 3

Racing Again

THOUGHTS OF RACING AGAIN

When Jimmy was able to talk, the first thing he said to us was, "I gotta get out of here...I have to race Friday." Can you believe it? Even at his weakest moments, his first thoughts were about racing! I was lost; I didn't know what to say. I knew he had no idea what happened. I believe that is how God protects someone from such trauma. All I could come up with was, "Jimmy you're in the hospital because you have a very bad cold and you need to get better before you can get out of here." There was a silence... My husband looked at me like... are you crazy? A cold with all these machines, a neck brace, he can't move...I looked at him like...I had to think fast! We could hear the nurses trying not to laugh. I could only imagine what Jimmy was thinking! Then Jim explained to Jimmy that he just finished his last race, and we were all done for the season. It worked. My husband Jim was quoted in a powerful interview entitled **Driver comes back from accident to race again** with the Point Park News Service of Point Park University's School of Communication in Pittsburgh, Pennsylvania, which was published on December 12, 2013, "I never had any doubts about him racing again," said his father, Jim Weller Jr. "Of course with your son doing this type of stuff, there is always a concern for his safety, but I never doubted whether he could do it or not."[6]

---

[6] **Driver comes back from accident to race again,** Point Park News Service of Point Park University's School of Communication, Pittsburgh, Pennsylvania, December 12, 2013 interview with Jim Weller.

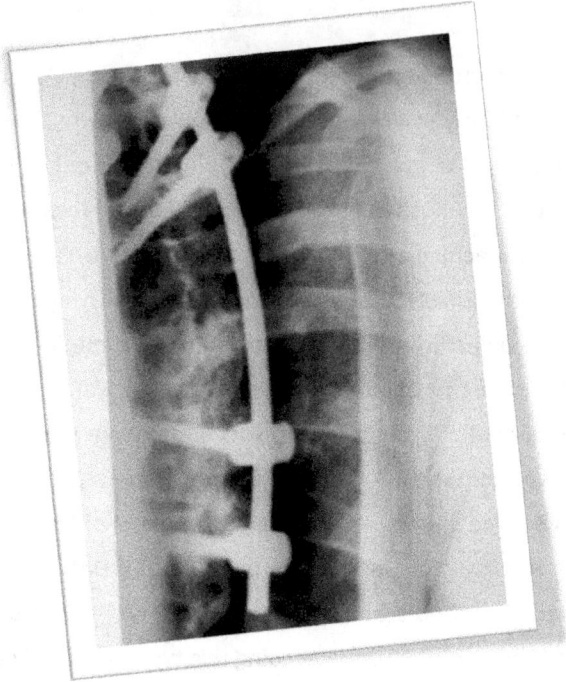

As Jimmy got stronger, he had to have the back surgery. He ended up with two rods and eight screws in his back. Dr. Finger did a tremendous job; we knew that there was a great risk of him being paralyzed if something went wrong; those compressed vertebrae were soooo close to the spinal cord. It seemed like the surgery lasted forever. Jim and I were still not going to give up. We knew he was going to be ok and, thank God, he was. Everything went well. Jimmy had a strong will to survive. Praise God. Another blessing!

TRUSTING GOD THROUGH THE PAIN – FAITH, FAMILY, and THE DESIRE TO RACE AGAIN

After recovering from the surgery, the next step was to the Rehab Hospital. The first day we were there, there was a problem and Jimmy ended up having immediate, emergency surgery on his neck. It was broken, the vertebrae had slipped...very critical and dangerous. You see, even when things get better in life, there may be a setback. Jim and I were devastated. It was a serious setback for Jimmy; we knew he was in so much pain. I was so scared; we knew how dangerous this was. He had just been through the back surgery. I can honestly say we had never stopped praying the whole time we had been there.

> We prayed for many different reasons; strength, courage, hope and, mostly, for thanksgiving and gratitude. I wasn't going to let my faith be shaken at this point, we couldn't give up.

The risk of Jimmy losing his life was hitting us again. I knew God would not leave us, not now; He'd been there the whole time.

I asked Jesus and Mary to hold Jimmy once again as they did the night of his accident.

I had to put him in God's hands, again, and I trusted Jesus. FOX Sports 1 reported, "Those closest to Jimmy credit his recovery to three simple factors: Faith, family, and his unwavering desire to race again."[7]

Dr. Finger was still at the hospital and was immediately ready to do the surgery. Thank God!!! But, this time it was different....Jimmy was awake...he knew something bad had just happened. He was in so much pain...I don't even think I can finish this right now, you see, just by writing this it all comes back, all the hurt of watching our son suffer and the look in his eyes as they took him away from us will never go away.

---

[7] FOX Sports 1 interview with the Weller family conducted on May 16, 2014.

I truly need to pause and praise God and praise Jesus for getting us through this. I need to take a few minutes to ask The Holy Spirit to help me go on as I have done so many times before.

Jim never left my side as we anxiously awaited the surgery to be done...we were again at a loss for words. He just quietly sat there holding me. I just hope I was as much comfort to him as he was for me. After hours of waiting we were told Jimmy's surgery had gone well.

Psalm 18:2 declares and decrees that,
"The Lord is my rock, and my fortress, and my deliverer; my God, my strength, in whom I will trust; ..."

God is so good to us, all of us. We must never forget even the smallest blessings The Lord gives us. We all need Him. We must always give back to God, someway or somehow to show Him how grateful we are for everything He does. You see, even though we have had many blessings through this, we have had some serious setbacks. And that's ok...we weren't alone and we knew it. We still gave Him thanks for everything.

The classic worship and praise song,
"Give Thanks", says,
"Give thanks with a grateful heart
Give thanks to the Holy One
Give thanks because He's given Jesus Christ, His Son"

After Jimmy recuperated from his neck surgery at the hospital, he was strong enough to go back to the Rehab Hospital to start therapy. Jim and I will never forget that first day there. We took Jimmy down to the physical therapy room in the wheel chair; he had lost 30 pounds by now; he wasn't very big to begin with. You could actually see his heart beating right through his chest. It broke my heart to see how frail he was. He couldn't stand up, he could hardly talk...yet, he was so happy.

You would never have known anything was wrong with him, only by looking at him. He was mentally doing better than both Jim and I. He was amazing! What an inspiration! We were with him 24/7 and loving every minute of it. We were able to be at every therapy, whether it was physical, cognitive, speech, or activities. It was great. Truly a blessing to be a part of Jimmy's healing.

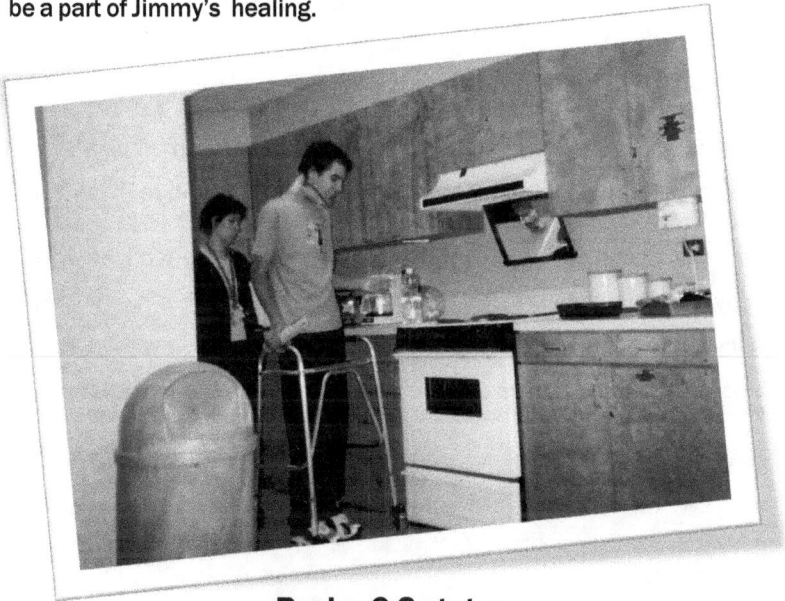

Psalm 6:2 states,
"Have mercy upon me, O Lord;
for I am weak: O Lord, heal me;"

WALK AGAIN EVEN IN PAIN

Now, his physical therapist, Carolyn, a very small, petite young lady did an amazing job of getting our son to walk again. When she lifted him out of the wheel chair and stood him up the first time, my husband and I looked at each other and all I could do was cry, my heart ached to see my son so weak.

Psalm 30:2 says,
"O Lord my God, I cried unto thee,
and thou hast healed me."

I couldn't imagine how she was ever going to get him to stand up, let alone walk again. It was that bad! But, she did! As small as she was, she was determined! Dear God, how will we ever be able to thank You!

Every day that went by, Jimmy got stronger and stronger. He was so happy! As I mentioned before, Jimmy was always such a happy person. He loved life. This was not going to hold him down for anything. He was so positive. He never gave up. Even as bad as he hurt during therapy, he would look at the two of us and just say, "it's ok", and fight even harder to finish. What an amazing young man! There are so many times, we had to pull our strength from him...if that makes any sense!

He wasn't giving up, because knew some day he was gonna race again.

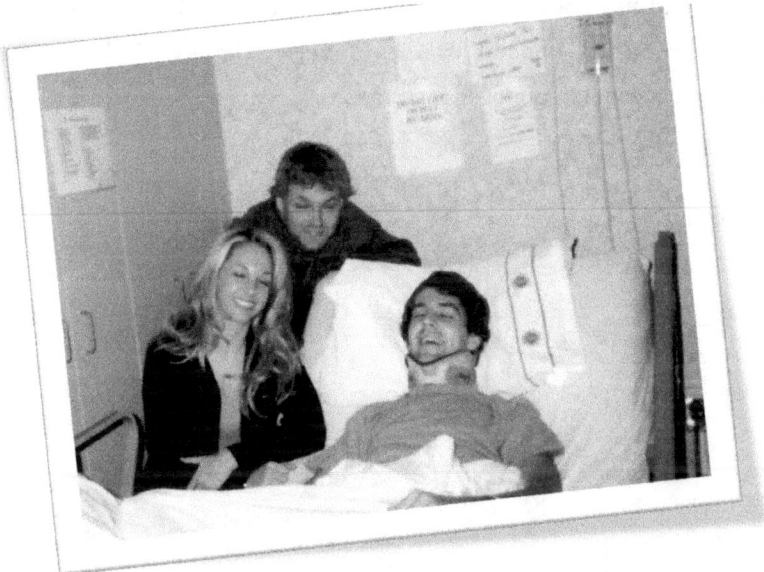

Jimmy at the Carolina's Rehabilitation with Crew Chief Jeff McCall and friend, Stacey Haynes

One day, he was really hurting; therapy really took a toll on him. It was a Sunday morning and they sent fliers to the patients rooms telling them what time the Sunday Service would be and that it would be in the therapy room. Each patient had their own room there, a hospital room with their own nurses. Jim and I were able to stay right in the room with Jimmy.

We were again blessed with amazing nurses who really loved their jobs!

When you're with these wonderful nurses for weeks at a time, you become like family. Nurse Katie Barton still continues to check on Jimmy and has become a very close friend to our whole family! Thank you dear, Katie and all who have helped Jimmy! God truly puts wonderful people in our lives for a reason!

TOUCHED BY THE TESTIMONY

When Jimmy found out about the Service, he had to go. I knew he was hurting, but there was no stopping him. He told us that if it wasn't for God, he wouldn't be here, and he had to go. We were so proud of Jimmy as we took him down in a wheel chair to the Church Service with some of the other patients. It was one of the most moving Services I had ever been to. The young man who talked at first was a survivor of a huge accident (who also was treated at that hospital) who now devotes his whole life to God. He touched all of us with his own testimony of what God can do.

Each patient had a remarkable recovery story...
ALL giving thanks to God.

There are some that may never physically walk again, but to them, just being in the presence of God was all they needed! Spiritually they were all walking again for they were deeply inspired by the powerful testimony.

Revelation 12:11 states,
"And they overcame him by the blood of the Lamb,
and by the word of their testimony;
and they loved not their lives unto the death."

Jimmy was progressing very fast and very well. It was now Thanksgiving and a very blessed Thanksgiving. They gave us the good news that Jimmy would be able to go out of the hospital only on that day for a few hours. We couldn't believe it. We were so happy.

When Jimmy's Crew Chief, Jeff, heard this, he planned a very special dinner at his house for us with his Mom and his son. When he got to the hospital to pick us up that day, I was so nervous having my son out for the first time that I was shaking; I was scared. I was hoping this was a good thing. I knew mentally it was good for all of us, but was Jimmy ready? Yes he was.... so ready that he thought we should go straight home and not go back to the hospital; he was healed. This made him fight even harder at therapy when we got back.

He was determined he was going home...soon.

Dinner was awesome; some of Jeff's racing friends came over to see Jimmy. Racing friends...Jimmy...it was perfect! It couldn't have been better for us, except Johnny wasn't able to get there on such quick notice. He spent Thanksgiving with Jim's family up home. I knew my in-laws would be there for him and make him feel just as important as Jimmy was feeling. It was very hard for me not to be able to spend the holiday with both my boys. We were always together as a family. I missed Johnny so much. He was still in school, which made it very hard for him to be there. Jim's wonderful parents would bring him down to North Carolina every weekend so he could see his brother...and us!

I enjoyed every moment I got to see Johnny. I hated it
when he had to leave. I had to do the only thing I knew,
and that was, I had to put him in God's hands.
You have to trust the Lord...and I did.

When we got back to the hospital, they told us that Jimmy was doing so
well that he could go home December 1st. What a wonderful Christmas
this would be! He had to reach a goal of walking by himself a certain
distance and be able to perform household tasks. And guess what? He
did it! We we're finally going home. He passed all of his tests; he was
now using a walker and MORE than ready to leave.

The three of us continued to pray day and night,
thanking God for everything that He had done to make
Jimmy the same person that he was before.

Thanking Him for all the blessings we had received. Jimmy was still so
happy. Never once did he complain, never once did he ask why. He was
so grateful to be here and he understood that it was by the Grace of God
that he would soon be living his life again; maybe not the same, but, still
living.

It was so exciting from then on.
What more could we ask for.
Jimmy was determined to walk on his own;
to be back the way he was. He inspired all of us.
He is truly a miracle.

Mike Hembree of *USA TODAY* Sports was so inspired by Jimmy that he wrote, "Weller was in intensive care for three weeks. The brain trauma locked him into a coma for the first week, and doctors induced a coma for another week as his battered body began the healing process. A screw was placed in his neck to support the fractured area, and two rods were inserted in his back where the spine had been fractured." Hembree also stated that, "Already thin, Weller lost another 40 pounds." Then Hembree quoted me saying, "He was all ribs and bones," Ronnie Weller said. "We could see his heart beating through his chest. They had to keep everything dark and quiet in his room. It was a good four weeks before his eyes opened, and they were still swollen. When he finally came out of the coma, I was holding his hand and he gripped my hand a little. Then when he talked, the first thing he told me was, 'I have to get out of here. I have to race Friday.' "[8]

---

[8] Mike Hembree, *USA TODAY* Sports section special, June 2, 2014.

They had told us ahead of time that most severe brain injury patients may have a complete change in personality. They could become very agitated and frustrated, things could be different. It didn't matter to us, we had our son back. I can honestly tell you, Jimmy never, ever, changed. He is still the wonderful, loving young man he always was. Truly, another blessing!

Everyone at the hospital was really proud of the hard work that Jimmy did and they were amazed at how positive he stayed through it all. They told us they truly believe that through all the prayers, his upbeat attitude and the support and love he received from everyone, and by having Jim and I there through the whole thing was truly why he was leaving there, let's say in record time. One therapist told us that no one with his injuries had ever left there in seven weeks, especially, doing as well as he was. A miracle; a true gift from God! I do have to say, racing was always in the back of his mind, he was not going to give up...he wanted to race again. His love for racing is what has driven him so hard at therapy...he knew someday he was going to be back in that car and race again.

Now I, on the other hand, could not even bare to think of him ever, ever getting into a race car again. This is something I truly wanted to put behind us. Knowing what was best for my son, I could never let him know how I felt. You see, to him, he should be racing. He loved it, and he literally lived it. He had no recollection of the accident...none. So to him, nothing changed, he was going racing. This is what had driven my son to get better so quickly. The passion he has for racing again is what I believe got us home in record time, and I was not going to let my son's dreams be shattered, surely not by me. I believed that God would be the judge of what Jimmy's future was going to be.

He was not going to give up...
He wanted to "Race Again".
His love for racing is what has driven him so hard at therapy...
He knew someday he was going to be back in that car and race again.

NASCAR driver and good friend, Dave Blaney, whether it was by himself or with his wonderful family, came to see Jimmy every week at the hospital. Dave will never realize how important all his visits were for Jimmy and for us.

He gave Jimmy the encouragement to work very hard. Jimmy wanted Dave to be proud of him. Dave was Jimmy's role model since he was kid; he was the best race car driver Jimmy knew, other than his Dad.

Seeing Dave was the only part of racing that Jimmy could connect with right now. We are so grateful for all that he and his family have done for us. Point Park News Service of Point Park University's School of Communication in Pittsburgh, Pennsylvania, stated that, "Weller credits veteran NASCAR Sprint Cup driver Dave Blaney as his mentor while growing up."[9]

The article goes on to state that, "What Jimmy has done has been incredible," said Blaney. "No one would think someone could come back from an accident like that. I'm always here to help him in any way I can."

---

[9] **Driver comes back from accident to race again,** Point Park News Service of Point Park University's School of Communication, Pittsburgh, Pennsylvania, December 12, 2013.

Jimmy and Dave Blaney, compliments of Howie Balis.

Jimmy was very anxious to get home, he missed his brother, his bed, his house, friends, everything. We were all so happy. We couldn't believe we were on our way.

Before we left, Father Larry, who had visited us once a week, had told us that he had witnessed a lot of things in his life, but no miracle like Jimmy's. He said he still remembered the day he anointed Jimmy in the intensive care unit...it didn't look good.

What he had witnessed was truly a Miracle.

He said he always enjoyed spending the time he could with Jimmy. Father Larry told us that he was inspired by how much faith a young man his age had. He said he would never forget what an impact Jimmy had made on him; and that Jimmy had taught him so much in such a short time.

1 Corinthians 9:24

Know ye not that they which run in a race run all, but one receiveth the prize? So run, that ye may obtain.

CHAPTER 4

God Will Never Give Up on You!

December 1st was finally here and we were going home.

Now you can imagine, John (15) was home for seven weeks, (except most weekends). And our godson, Chris (20), who is definitely like one of our own kids, was staying at the house with John and all of our dogs. We had no idea what to expect when we got home. Was our house going to look the same? Did they remember to feed the dogs? But you know what, if the house was a wreck and the dogs were skinnier, that was ok, it didn't matter; John was safe, and we were bringing our son home! We would all be together again. Something that October 13th could have changed forever.

FAITH AND FAMILY CARING, SHARING, AND BEARING

It's funny how when you come that close to losing your child, the whole world stops...nothing else matters...only God and your children. We would never have made it through this without our faith, the faith that we as a family had shared so deeply.

As we reached the driveway with so much anticipation, we saw banners, signs, balloons welcoming Jimmy home. Jimmy was in his glory! We all were.

We came to find out that the night before, family and race friends got together and had quite the party; making it a wonderful welcoming home for Jimmy. Food, baked goods, everything. It was awesome. Still can't thank everyone enough for all their love and support. John and Chris had, to our surprise, everything in order!

And yet...another blessing!!!

We couldn't get to the house quick enough! When I looked at our house... I cried!!! The house was completely decorated for Christmas; lights on every bush, every tree, wreaths on all the windows. John knows how much Christmas means to me, and to see all that just added to all my excitement. We were all overwhelmed, words cannot describe the joy we were all feeling. The two boys worked so hard to pull this off. I couldn't hold back the tears; these were tears of joy. The entire seven weeks of all the trauma, the tears, the sadness and the fear of never seeing our son again was all behind us. We were home. I was so proud of John and Chris... the house was clean, the dogs were alive, everything was good!

Can you imagine how John felt having his brother and his mom and dad home...finally! I can only imagine the pain he had felt in his heart every time he had to leave his brother every weekend. It was a long and trying seven weeks!

As we reached the front door, Johnny immediately came out to the car to help get his brother out and into the house. What an amazing show of unselfish love!

**Thank you God for the love that my family
has for one another and for allowing
my family to be together again.
This was truly our best Christmas ever!**

John was so much aware of Jimmy's injuries that he became overprotective of his brother. He wasn't going to lose him again. When he was at home, he devoted what little time he had (school and work kind of got in the way) to help in Jimmy's recovery. We still had a lot of work to do at home with Jimmy. We had to keep strengthening him, not only physically, but, mentally. The house had to be made accessible for the wheelchair and the walker...and you know what? It was, without hesitation! John would walk Jimmy up and down the hall, help get his food, he did whatever it took to make Jimmy feel as if nothing had changed. John even made sure that Jimmy did his exercises to help challenge his brain; he really worked with Jimmy. He was amazing! I couldn't have been more proud him.

Jimmy had to finish six weeks of therapy at Hillside Rehabilitation Hospital here in Ohio. And once again...yet another blessing...he was done in three weeks. He was determined to race again! I know that Jesus healed Jimmy's brain completely; you see, Jimmy had to pass certain tests here, too before he was released. And he did! There is nothing wrong with his brain, I can say that because after he took the last cognitive test and we got in the car to leave,...he said "Mom, Mary (the therapist), didn't know that on the one test I could see all the answers as she turned the page." I laughed. I said, "You know, Jimmy, if you knew enough to cheat...your brain is working just fine! Not that I promote cheating, but that was pretty impressive!"

Now there are a few things that Jimmy struggles with from the accident, but nothing that God has given us that we can't handle.

Thank you Jesus for healing our son.

During those seven weeks that we spent in Charlotte, Chad Wagner, a very dear friend who we love like he is our own son, did so much to help. He had arranged to have all the cards sent to the hospital, he had t-shirts made up with Jimmy's racing on it and sold them to collect money to help with the hospital expenses. To this day, I am truly amazed at what a remarkable young man he is and all the effort he put into all of this, for which we are so grateful. We will never forget what he has done. We love you, Chad!

You see, at the race tracks, if a driver got hurt they would take up a collection and present it to the family. Since Jimmy's was the very last race of the season, Chad thought of another way to help. Linda Barlow who is a big fan of my husband's and Jimmy's also wanted to do something to help. So Chad and she worked on giving a benefit for Jimmy. What an undertaking...they got together with Quaker Steak & Lube in Sharon, PA and put on one amazing benefit. It was held in

January because they were hoping that by then Jimmy would be able to attend...and he did! He wasn't going to miss out on a good time and be with all his friends and family. I will never forget that day... the three of us walked in behind Jimmy as he walked in using the walker, wearing the neck brace and looking as frail as you can imagine. He was very weak, but determined to be there. He walked in with the biggest smile ever!!! It had to be one of the happiest days of his life and ours, too! Wow...to walk in and see so many people standing there giving Jimmy the biggest applause ever was truly a blessing to our family. One that we will never forget...ever!!! We would really like to thank all of you who attended, all who donated their time and wonderful items donated for the auction.

Thank you to all of you and may God bless you now and forever! Special thanks and blessings to Chad, Linda and Quaker Steak for doing an outstanding job on the benefit!

As Jimmy continues to recover, he remains as happy and positive as ever. It's as if the accident was only a part of what his life had to be, and he accepted that; he never looked back. He even has gone as far as to say one day,

"Ya know, Mom, I don't know how to say this, but I am glad that this happened to me and not to someone who didn't believe in God because how would they have ever made it through this."

I stopped and just looked at my son. I didn't know what to say. Every time you think you couldn't be any more proud of your children (like the way Johnny took care of Jimmy), something like this happens and your heart just grows a thousand times larger with love for your child. Is that possible? I thought I loved my boys with all my heart already.

I guess there is no end to how much love we have. To this day, I am still so in awe of what Jimmy said. What incredible faith!!!

I know that Jimmy is here for a reason. There is something God needs him to do. He spared his life, and I believe my son knows that he is only here by the Grace of God.

Jimmy always has a good time talking with Johnny D at the Chevy Stage.

FOCUSING ON RACING AGAIN

Jimmy and I had a lot of talks about life and how some things would change because of his accident. I could sense that he was troubled by something; I think he was beginning to question the fact that he might not ever be able to race again. This broke my heart. It's like his dreams; and hopes were being taken away and going toward some other direction. He told me that he had been praying that if God did not want him to ever race again, would He please guide him in the direction he needed to go. He just needed an answer on what to do. His heart was truly into racing, but he loved God so much that he would do whatever God wanted him to do.

Things started moving very quickly. Once Jimmy was checked over by the doctors and knew he was completely healed over and stronger than he was before the accident, he started focusing on racing again with a greater passion than ever before.

Jimmy's faith is so strong and his love for God is immeasurable.

I truly believe that because Jimmy was willing to give up his dream and do whatever God had planned for him is the reason God has given him his dream back.

I believe that when we put God first, everything else just falls into place.

Jimmy is a true follower of Christ. I am so very proud of my son, both my boys! Jimmy and John, they are partners forever. They both truly love The Lord, which is all I ever hoped for.

iv

I'm sure you can tell where this is heading...Jimmy did get back into the race car. He started out racing the first few races in his Dad's other Modified. Point Park News Service of Point Park University's School of Communication in Pittsburgh, Pennsylvania, wrote, "Weller has not only regained his health, but he also returned to racing, rising to NASCAR Camping World Truck Series fame."

I knew he was safe, Jim's crew chief and our dear friend, John Corbin, would never put him in an unsafe car, I knew that! Sure, I was nervous and scared, but I was ok with this...I had to be...this was God's will. I'll be honest, I watched the only way I could...with my eyes closed!

The Kansas City Star reported in an article entitled **Rookie Jimmy Weller overcomes horrific crash and begins career in Truck Series** by Randy Covitz on May 9, 2014, "When Weller, of Hubbard, Ohio, returned to racing in 2006 in big block Modifieds, his parents were understandably apprehensive." The article went on to quote Jimmy who said; "They were trying to get me to slow down. My dad actually walked on the track to slow me down a little bit, and I drove around him slow and went quick around the other corner."[10]

Ten years later, after experiencing different levels of racing, Jimmy has been given a wonderful opportunity racing in the NASCAR Camping World Truck Series and The Xfinity Series, formally the NASCAR Nationwide Series. What a blessing from God! Jimmy told FOX Sports concerning involvement in NASCAR racing, "That's always a dream...to get up to this level...and to get to run a nationwide, It's...that was a dream. Like right now I'm kind of caught up in everything trying to make it work. When I'm older, and I kind of look back at life, I'm going to go, this is where I was. This is an awesome deal."[11]

I Corinthians 9:24 states,
"Know ye not that they which run in a race run all, but one receiveth the prize? So run, that ye may obtain."

---

[10] Kansas City Star, Rookie Jimmy Weller overcomes horrific crash and begins career in Truck Series by Randy Covitz, May 9, 2014
[11] FOX Sports 1 interview with Jimmy Weller conducted on May 16, 2014.

v

Mike Hembree of *USA TODAY* Sports wrote in the article entitled, ***Jimmy Weller back at full speed after terrible crash***, "Almost 10 years later, the Jimmy Weller who pops out of a race-car hauler in the garage at Charlotte Motor Speedway looks nothing like the shell of that 18-year-old. He is bright and handsome, funny and engaging, eager to run the next lap and generally a bundle of energy." Hembree also stated that, "Many of those around him celebrate the fact that he is alive. That he races at nearly 200 mph is beyond imagination."[12]

Thank you Heavenly Father

FOX Sports asked Jimmy the thought provoking question, "...what is inside of race car drivers that makes them want to keep getting on the race track and chasing their dreams?" As Jimmy was preparing to race at NASCAR he answered FOX Sports, "To be honest with you, I really don't know. In. It's awesome, just how much fun it is. They always say, you know, when racing's in your blood, you can't get out. And my joke is, you know, no matter how hard you get hit in the head, you,...you can't get it out of your head. Just something that it keeps bringing you back. It's the adrenaline, it's the excitement and, and just the competition, man. It, it brings you back."[13]

We're not sure what the future will hold for Jimmy's racing career, but as for now, we thank God every day for giving us back our son; we thank Jesus for healing him, and I thank Jesus and Mary for holding our son that night and for letting me be a witness to the most beautiful sight and for letting Jimmy live his dream all over again. It may not be in the Sprint

---

[12] Mike Hembree, *USA TODAY* Sports section special, June 2, 2014.
[13] FOX Sports 1 interview with Jimmy Weller conducted on May 16, 2014.

car which is where his heart was, but he is really happy and grateful where he is today.

**Jimmy truly owes his life to God.
We all do.**

---

vi

As for me; Jimmy being in a race car again was truly not what I wanted, but I believe it's what God wanted for him. I pray a lot while Jimmy is on the track; first and most important for his safety, and then I ask God to help me...help me to get through every time when he gets in the car, every time I hear the sound of the engine as he starts the car...especially, every time he's involved in a crash...help me Lord...I can't do this alone.

His first race back I literally broke down and cried...I was so scared. There was no way I could watch...I was sick. I knew the worst thing that I could do was to let Jimmy sense even the slightest change in my enthusiasm for him racing again. You see, my boys and I are so close that if they even suspected anything was wrong, they would do anything they could to help me. That was not good right now; I know how Jimmy would have reacted to this, he would have been more concerned about how this affected me, which I knew would have went with him behind the wheel of that car.

No way was I going to jeopardize my son's well being on that race track. I ran to the truck and went inside where I could be alone; I literally broke down...I cried so hard...I seriously couldn't breathe. I got down on my knees, and I begged God to take hold of me and help me...I just wanted to die. I always knew it was going to be hard, and I knew my faith was going to help me through; then why was I so weak, so sick? Did my faith weaken? Was I losing control? How could I have let this happen? I couldn't do this to God; after everything he did for me and my family? I was ashamed of myself. Did I let God down? Did I lose my trust in Jesus?

After spending an hour there alone, crying and desperately praying to God, I realized I wasn't alone; Jesus had been there with me the whole time. He listened. I was reacting as a protective Mom, a mom who loves her child very much. I was only reacting to that very trauma that I witnessed on October 13th. I prayed for strength, I prayed for courage; and I prayed that I could give Jimmy all the support he needed. I knew all along Jimmy was going to be ok, God showed me that, and He led Jimmy to where he should be.

It was me...was I going to be ok? Could I make it through? That time alone I had with Our Lord showed me that He was there for me, He wasn't going to leave me go through this alone. He comforted me.

He gave me the strength and courage to go back out there...and...I cheered my son on.

I watched that race, every bit of it. Sure it was hard for me Jimmy's first few years back into racing, but with the presence of Jesus and Mary, I made it! And as every new season starts, I can only do the right thing and that is to put him in God's hands and trust in Jesus as I have always done.

You see, he is not only my child; he is God's child. He's my child temporarily, he's God's child for eternity. Not mine – His.

REMEMBERING PADRO

Jimmy was coming home from work one day to get ready to head to the race track when he saw this little dog in the middle of road. Naturally, he stopped and when he opened the door this little dog jumped in. He was so scrawny, undernourished and loaded with fleas, but had enough energy to hop in with Jimmy. Jimmy checked the nearest homes on the street, but no one had ever seen this adorable little dog before. I get this phone call from Jimmy to meet him at the race shop telling me he has a surprise he wanted me to see... I was to bring a bowl and milk. Knowing my son, it could have been any little critter!

As I pulled up to the race shop, there was Jimmy holding this adorable little dog and I knew by the looks of him I had better get him straight to the vets office. I hurried up and took Padro, which is the name Jimmy gave him, to Dr. Troy Parks, our Vet, who is so used to us bringing in dogs we have rescued. At one point, we had five rescued dogs, we are now down to three. He immediately got rid of the fleas, gave him shots and basically saved his life, although he says that we did for giving Padro a wonderful home and lots of love!

I raced back to the shop with our new dog, Padro and we all jumped in the hauler and headed to the races. That was the beginning of Padro's racing career!

My little Padro was an Angel sent down from Heaven at a time when I needed him the most. I do believe God sent him to me when Jimmy got back into racing for a reason. God always knows the best way to heal us and knowing that is was going to be a scary road ahead with Jimmy on the race track again, He gave me comfort in having Padro there for me to hold on to.....a sense of security. He was always right there with me at almost every race until he died peacefully September 28, 2014. Thank you Heavenly Father for putting him in my life just at the right time. I miss him very much!

REMEMBERING PADRO

Padro rode on Jimmy's shoulders most of the time when we drove to the races in our hauler.

REMEMBERING PADRO

Padro

REMEMBERING PADRO

After the accident Padro was my security blanket.

REMEMBERING PADRO

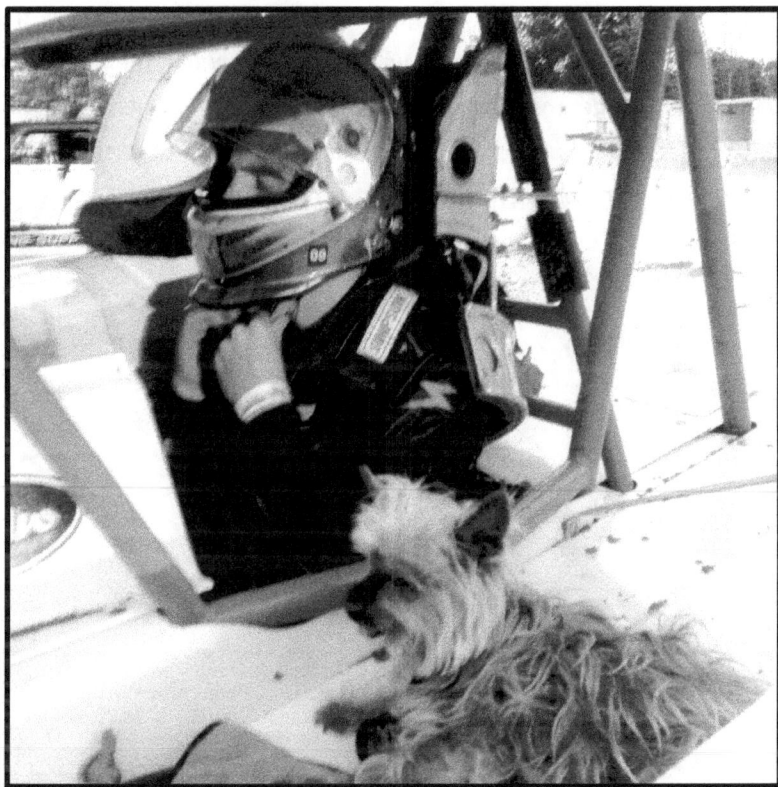

Jimmy and Padro

Jimmy stated in the interview with Point Park News Service of Point Park University's School of Communication in Pittsburgh, Pennsylvania, that, "My family members are my biggest supporters. From being at all the races, helping me keep my head up no matter how bad the night was, working hard to get me to where I am today. It sounds cliché, but you're only as good as the people around you. I have been blessed to have awesome people helping me in every step of my career."[14]

---

[14] **Driver comes back from accident to race again,** Point Park News Service of Point Park University's School of Communication, Pittsburgh, Pennsylvania, December 12, 2013 interview with Jimmy Weller.

Jimmy spending quality time with the kids
in the community. Basketball first,
then talking about chasing their dreams.

Jimmy has had the privilege of speaking to confirmation classes, retreats, church groups and schools sharing his truly miraculous story. He honestly believes, as we all do, he is only here by the Grace of God and that God has a plan for him. He truly wants to give back to God as much as he possibly can. He has plans to continue sharing his faith and his story to other churches and groups in the future. When he is finished speaking, he leaves them with this:

"Please don't give up on God, I'm proof
that God will never give up on you."

In the circle of life, there are many roads that we must travel to end up on the path that the Lord has provided for us. Only God knows what the future holds for us and what we have to go through to get there. It is that awesome faith that we have that allows us to truly know it comes from Him.

Jimmy talking to the kids about having faith & chasing your dreams.

This is from a bookmarker that one of my CCD students gave me years ago, (I had the privilege of teaching CCD for our Church for 12 years), and I truly believe it applies to everything that has happened me:

I will always thank the Lord;
I will never stop praising Him.
I will praise Him for what he has done;
may all who are oppressed
listen and be glad!
Proclaim with me the Lord's greatness;
let us praise His name together!

I prayed to the Lord,
and He answered me;
He freed me from all my fears.
The oppressed look to Him
and are glad;
they will never be disappointed..
I was a nobody, but I prayed,
and the Lord saved me
from all my troubles.

His angels guard those who
have reverence for the Lord
and rescues them from danger.

Find out for yourself how good
the Lord is. Happy are those
who find safety with Him.

Psalm 34:1-8

Hebrews 12:1

Wherefore seeing we also are compassed about

with so great a cloud of witnesses, let us lay

aside every weight, and the sin which doth so

easily beset us, and let us run with patience

the race that is set before us,

CHAPTER 5
Never Give Up

Never Give Up

Just like any other family, we continue to have trials of our own, but nothing The Lord can't get us through! When racing season is finished for the year, our family enjoys any kind of snow activity.

I myself, absolutely love the snow, not sure if it's the right thing to do, but I sometimes ask God to bless me with lots of it!!!   I would love it if it would snow all year!

In 2009, we were on our annual ski trip out West, which that year was at Snowmass, CO. My husband and son, John were snowboarding and Jimmy and I were skiing. Jimmy loved snowboarding, but because of his injuries and all the hardware he has in his neck and back, he can only casual ski... Dr's orders! Try telling a race car driver he can only go slow skiing! I continually have to remind him to slow down as he's zooming past me on the slopes! For some reason I always let them go down the mountain first so I can be the last one in case someone falls and needs me.....that's the Mom in me! Oh don't get me wrong, I have taken many falls on those mountains! Well, this trip was different.

It was our first day, first run and we were at the top of the mountain when the snow picked up and was almost like blizzard conditions. The snow starting coming down so fast and so heavy that it started to worry me because I didn't want Jimmy to fall.

He and I were the last to get off the lift because Jim and Johnny were long gone on those snowboards. I started to go first, only God knows why and I thank him to this day that I did. Jimmy was behind me at this point, probably waiting to see if I fell because I always do regardless if there is snow or not! The snow was coming down so hard and heavy that I could not get control of my skis when my legs started to slide apart, kind of like a split which I have never been able to do in my entire life. I was picking up speed, fearing for my life because I didn't know what was going to happen when I finally heard three cracks in my right knee and somehow I fell flat on my back. My legs were bent so that my feet were almost at my shoulders.

I was in so much pain that I must have been in shock by the time Jimmy got to me.

I kept trying to get my skis unhooked, but there was no way I could reach my boot to unhook them. It would have been so much easier if I would have fallen and the skis would have come out of the bindings. It was something like out of a movie: it was snowing hard, blizzard conditions, the way I seen it, so bitter cold and not one person in sight!

Jimmy literally had to lift my foot up out of the snow, unhook the skis and straighten my legs to bring them to their normal positions.

Oh my gosh!!! The pain was unbearable! Thank you God for having Jimmy right there by my side. When I think about it, which I try not to, if my family would have gone down the mountain ahead of me, I would have been stranded there, probably passed out from the pain and most likely froze to death...ok, that part I might have exaggerating a bit! Still, I thank God that it didn't happen! I do believe our Guardian Angels are with us ALL the time! If you knew how clumsy I am, my Guardian Angel is never going to catch a break!

Jimmy immediately called Jim and Johnny for help. They had just reached the bottom of the mountain when they were able to get his message. Jimmy told them to send up someone from the ski patrol because there was no way he could move me. While we were waiting, we had only seen one other person on the mountain who skied right beside us, actually, he was out of control and didn't stop. We knew by the way he was struggling to get down the mountain, he wasn't going to be able to help us. We thought we had troubles, this poor guy looked like he was a beginner fearing for his life.....Jimmy and I both looked at each other and wished we could have helped him!

I can't quit thanking God that the ski patrol
was able to find right where we were.

It was about a half hour until they reached us and by this time, Jimmy and I were about frozen! I do believe my feet were starting to get frostbite. Anyone who has ever skied before knows those boots are not very comfortable and not warm at all!

Since Jimmy's accident, I guess I have become more protective of my children and probably always will be. I was more worried about Jimmy than I was about myself. I kept asking him, are you ok, and are you warm enough? I was willing to give him my coat, my gloves just so he could stay warm. He was so darn cute, he's like," Mom....I'm ok, honest" and kept trying to help me.

As the rescue team starts to help lift me up...... I looked at them with this painful, confused look on my face and thought...... I'm not quite ready to go down the mountain on this plastic shell thing they brought up. What happened to the snowmobiles that I have seen people being taken down the mountain on? For me, I have to lay on this shell and the girl has to attach a rope to her poles so she could ski me down....nooo way!

I may have been in shock, but I thank God I was still aware of this scary and bumpy ride that was ahead me.

I guess if I was going to get down that mountain and get out of this pain, it was my only choice. And lo and behold, as we are trying to gently go down the hill, me lying head first on this thing, she falls!

Thank God she did not let go of the rope, I would have been down that mountain like Chevy Chase on the saucer in Christmas Vacation!

When we finally got to the bottom of the hill to the medical center, Jim and Johnny were waiting there for us. I don't think they ever imagined it was that bad! The worst was yet to come.....my feet were so bitter cold and swollen that they couldn't get my ski boots off, which are very hard to get off in the first place. I am not a violent person at all, but when they started pulling the boots off, I literally jumped up and was going to slug the nurse. It wasn't his fault, but the pain had taken over!

Both legs were really messed up, but thank God I wear a brace on my left knee when I ski from yet another ski injury, which somehow protected it. I know how! Just to mention, I do have a herniated disc in my neck from trying to snowboard....I love skiing!

I tore the MCL on the right knee and tore the cartilage in the socket of the right hip joint. After 4 years of struggling with pain, two surgeries and some pretty extensive therapy, I was finally back to living my live normally again. And the reason for that is because I never gave up! I never quit praying and asking for God's help through it all. Jesus healed me! The pain was so bad, but I continued to go to every race with Jimmy, leaving on Thurs and getting back on Sunday. I knew that if God allowed me to wake up the next day, I would do everything I could to thank Him.

I had to keep moving knowing how hard my son worked to get back to the life that God had given him again, I couldn't give up.

I couldn't let this destroy my life. I won't lie, there were times when it was so painful that I just wanted to fall asleep and not wake up.

But God had given me the strength like He has done so many times before to keep going.

With lots of prayers, determination and believe it or not, two more pretty bad falls after that and more therapy, I am still going! When things get you down and things get tough, please know that The Lord will never let you go through it alone, He's always there.

Thank you God for all Your love.
Thank you Jesus for healing me again!

Race Again

ABOUT NASCAR DRIVER
JIMMY WELLER

"Once racing is in your blood, you can't get away from it." Very few racecar drivers' stories prove that statement more truly than that of Jimmy

Weller's. After a successful, but short, career in go karts on both asphalt and dirt, Jimmy began racing Big Block Modifieds at Sharon Speedway at the age of 15. After two full seasons in the Modifeds, which resulted in three regional awards, one touring series victory and Top 10 finishes in each track's end of the year points standings,

Jimmy followed his childhood dreams of sitting behind the wheel of a 410 Sprint Car.

In 2004 Jimmy discovered Sprint cars fit into his driving style perfectly and his six total wins for his rookie year proved that he was suited best for Sprint cars. Jimmy also won one point's championship and one national level award. Although his year started out on a good note, things quickly went sour in the USAC Sprint Car race at The Dirt Track at Lowe's Motor Speedway in Charlotte, North Carolina. While racing for the lead in his heat race, Jimmy caught a rut entering turn one and flipped violently into the outside fence.

During one of the flips, Jimmy's head made direct contact with one of the fence support posts, causing Jimmy to lose consciousness and fracturing both his neck and back. Jimmy was in a comatose state for two weeks and underwent different surgeries to help heal the fractures to his neck and back.

With a pin in his neck and two rods in his back, the Grace of God had Jimmy walking out of the hospital seven short weeks later.

After meetings with world renowned doctors, Jimmy knew it was safe to get back into a racecar after taking the 2005 season off. Due to the dangerous risks involved in racing Sprint cars, Jimmy's doctors advised him not to get behind the wheel of a Sprint car again.

Jimmy's dreams of racing Sprint cars may have been shattered, but he was still very eager and thankful to get back into a car and begin chasing his dreams again.

Jimmy's return to racing was in the Big Block Modifieds at Sharon Speedway before switching midway through the 2006 season to the asphalt Late Models at Lake Erie Speedway. With success at the local tracks and with the ASA Challenge Series.

Jimmy made the move to North Carolina to race out of Dave Blaney's shop in the PASS South Late Model Series. One win and two full seasons later, Jimmy and team made the jump to the NASCAR K&N Pro Series East in 2012. Jimmy achieved 11th place in the end of the year points standings in his rookie year. 2013 started off with racing the K&N Series before taking the leap to the NASCAR Camping World Truck Series. A handful of races were run in the Truck Series in 2013 in preparation of a larger schedule to be run in 2014.

2001- Made six starts at Sharon Speedway in the Big Block Modifieds at the age of 15

2002- Won the Lernerville Speedway Rookie of the Year and the Western Pennsylvania Rookie of the Year for Dirt awards in the Big Block Modifieds

2003- Won first career Big Block Modified event at Wayne County Speedway with the BRP Modified Tour. Was awarded the Twin State Auto Racing Club's Most Improved Driver

2004- In his rookie year of 410 Sprint Cars, won two feature events- one at Lernerville Speedway and one at Sharon Speedway. Was voted Top 25 Under 25 in the nation for the Sprint Car and Midget magazine. Was joined with dad in being awarded the Milestone Award at Lernerville Speedway for both winning their features on the same night; Dad in the Big Block Modifieds and Jimmy in the 410 Sprint Cars. Won four of six feature events and the points championship in the inaugural season of the Green Flag Sprint Cars at Sharon Speedway. Sustained critical injuries in the USAC Sprint Car event at the Dirt Track at Lowe's Motor Speedway, forcing the sitting out of the **2005 season.**

2006- Began the season racing the Big Block Modifieds at Sharon Speedway before switching to asphalt Late Models at Lake Erie Speedway midway through the year

2007- Won feature at Lake Erie Speedway in the Late Models

2008- Won the finale for the Late Models at the World Series of Stock Car Racing at New Smyrna Speedway along with a feature event at Lake Erie Speedway

2009- Won opening night in the Late Models at the World Series of Stock Car Racing at New Smyrna Speedway. In late July, made the move to North Carolina to race the PASS South Late Model tour

2010- Won the 150 lap, PASS South Series tour event at South Boston Speedway

2011- Continued racing the PASS Series and made his initial Nascar K&N Pro Series East start at New Hampshire Motor Speedway and recorded a 14th place finish

2012- Finished 11th in the overall points standings and 3rd in the Rookie of the Year points standings, recording two Top 10's in the Nascar K&N Pro Series East

2013- Began the season racing the K&N Series before making a handful of starts in the Nascar Camping World Truck Series

2014- Compelled on a limited schedule in the Camping World Truck Series

2015 – Jimmy Weller races in the NASCAR Xfinity Series Schedule.

IF YOU WOULD LIKE TO EMAIL JIMMY OR THE TEAM, FEEL FREE TO DROP US A LINE AT JWELLERRACING@GMAIL.COM

Jimmy Weller III races again and leads a pack of trucks during the Lucas Oil 200 Camping World Truck Series race, recently at Dover International Speedway.

www.jimmyweller.com/

www.facebook.com/JWellerRacing

www.instagram.com/JWellerRacing/

Veronica "Ronnie" Weller

Veronica "Ronnie" Weller was born and raised in Youngstown, OH. As a child she attended Saints Cyril & Methodius Catholic Church and School before moving to Hubbard, OH when she was thirteen. She graduated from Hubbard High School in 1975 and now resides in Liberty Township, Ohio with her husband, Jim, and their two sons, Jimmy and John, three dogs and one ferocious cat!

For 11 years, she enjoyed teaching CCD for Saints Bernadette's Church in Masury, Ohio. CCD, (Confraternity of Christian Doctrine). CCD was the religion class she taught to children who weren't in Catholic Schools where religion was a main subject. These classes brought them to a better understanding of their Faith and helped them prepare and make their Sacraments. The classes were held one night a week (or on Sunday's between Masses) during the school year.

She has a passion for volunteering and helping people. Over the years she has spent time volunteering at the Northeast Ohio Adoption Services in Howland, Ohio for their two annual fund raising events and The Ronald McDonald House in Youngstown. She also supports The Rescue Mission of Mahoning Valley in Youngstown, Ohio, and The Association of The Miraculous Medal in Perryville, MO, with her prayer requests and donations.

When her and her family are not at a race track, she enjoys snow skiing and road trips across the country on the motorcycle with her husband and friends.

Her love for Jesus and her family is what she cherishes most in life.

RACE AGAIN

The Power of Faith and Family

Ecclesiastes 9:11

I returned, and saw under the sun, that the race is not to the swift, nor the battle to the strong, neither yet bread to the wise, nor yet riches to men of understanding, nor yet favour to men of skill; but time and chance happeneth to them all.

1 Corinthians 9:24

Know ye not that they which run in a race run all, but one receiveth the prize? So run, that ye may obtain.

Hebrews 12:1

Wherefore seeing we also are compassed about with so great a cloud of witnesses, let us lay aside every weight, and the sin which doth so easily beset us, and let us run with patience the race that is set before us,

RACE AGAIN

The Power of Faith and Family

 **RACE AGAIN**

The Power of Faith and Family

 **RACE AGAIN**

The Power of Faith and Family

RACE AGAIN

The Power of Faith and Family

Race Again by Ronnie Weller

Published by

Mackey Productions
"Catch the Vision of Victory & Never Give Up"

Available From
Mackey Productions
RACE AGAIN
By Ronnie Weller

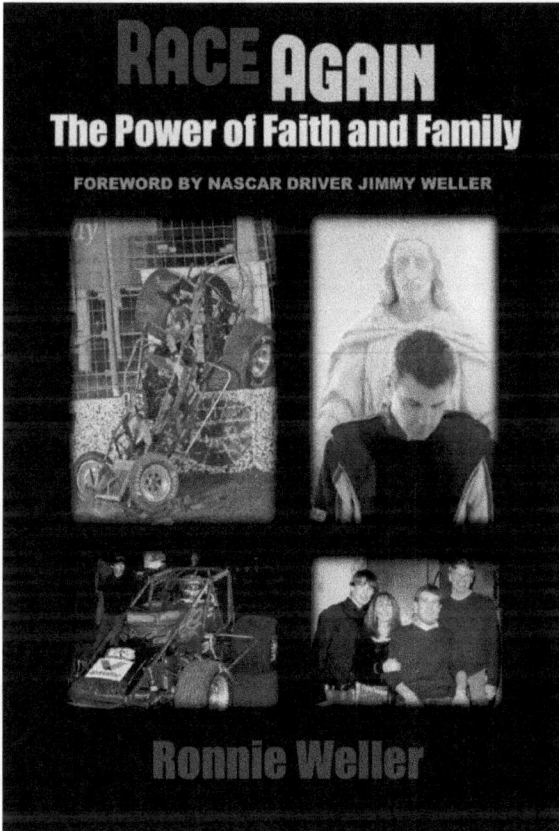

List Price: $12.99

ISBN-13: 978-0692409060
ISBN-10: 0692409068
Library of Congress Control Number: 2015938194

Also Available From Mackey Productions
A MINDSET FOR CHANGE
by Arthur Mackey

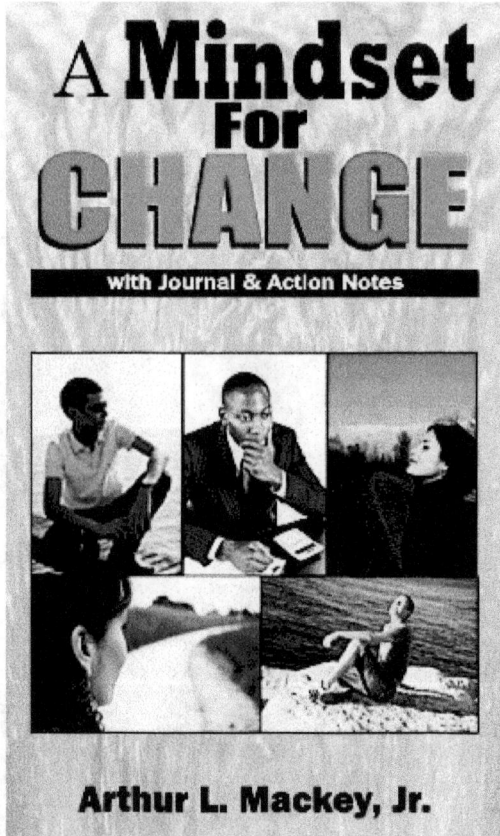

A **Mindset** For
CHANGE
with Journal & Action Notes

Arthur L. Mackey, Jr.

List Price: **$9.99**

ISBN-13: 978-1453615874
ISBN-10: 1453615873
BISAC: Body, Mind & Spirit / Inspiration & Personal Growth

Also Available From Mackey Productions

THE CALL TO COMMITMENT
by Arthur Mackey

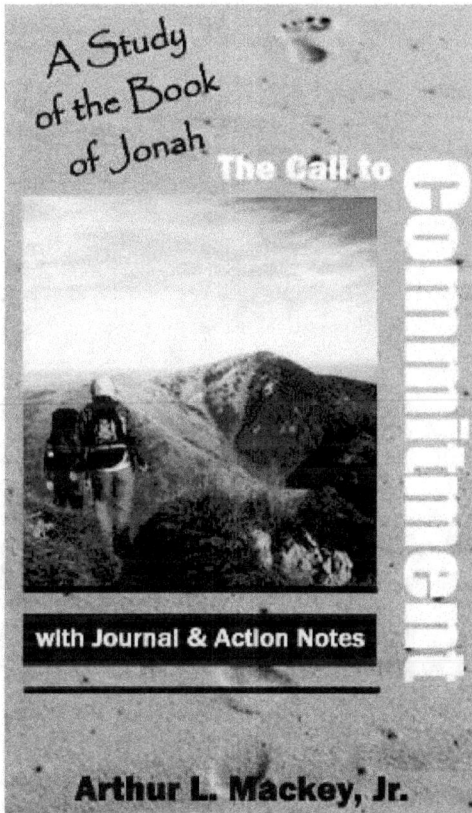

List Price: **$11.99**

ISBN-13: 978-1453686652
ISBN-10: 1453686657
BISAC: Religion / Christian Life / Spiritual Growth

Also Available From Mackey Productions
CHOSEN TO BE A SOLDIER
by Arthur Mackey

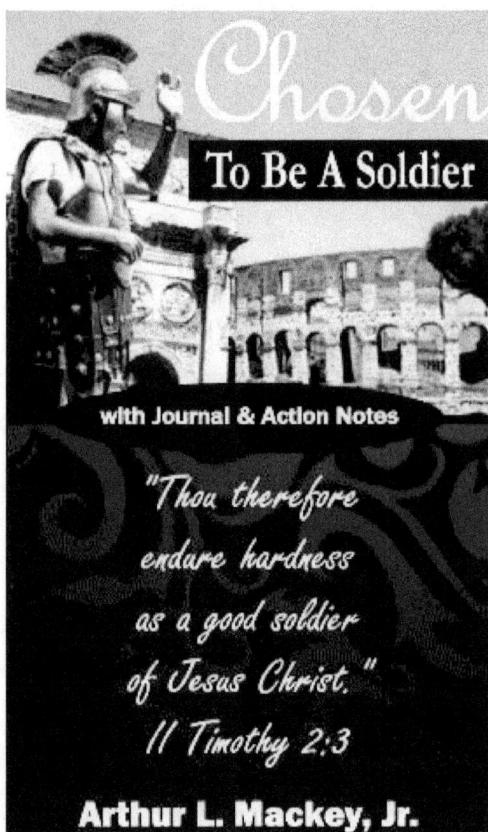

List Price: **$10.99**

ISBN-13: 978-1453700655
ISBN-10: 145370065X
BISAC: Religion / Christian Life / Spiritual Growth

CONTACT INFORMATION

To contact the Author, Ronnie Weller
and NASCAR Driver Jimmy Weller

for television, radio, and or print interviews, or speaking engagements.

Please write them at

P.O. Box 214

Hubbard, OH 44425

---

[i] Photo by John Weller

[ii] Crash photos by Kevin Thorne Photography

[iii] Photo by Joe Secka

[iv] Photo by John Hinely Photography

[vv] Photo by Scott Schilke

[vi] ibid.

[vii] ibid.

[viii] Photo by Ashleigh Aungst at the Providence Church of God, Locust, North Carolina

[ix] Skiing pictures by Jim Weller. Wendy Hughes is the first picture with Ronnie.

[x] Poster art, "On The Brick" by Seth Tysick

[xi] Photo by Scott Schilke